DAVID GOODE

❧ EIGHT SONNETS ❧

BY
FRANCIS WARNER

BARITONE AND PIANO

COLIN SMYTHE LTD
2016

Published 2016 by Colin Smythe Limited
38 Mill Lane, Gerrards Cross, Buckinghamshire, SL9 8BA
www.colinsmythe.co.uk

The publisher expresses gratitude that this publication has been made possible
by a generous grant in appreciation of the poet who was the sponsor's tutor
for the three years that the sponsor was an undergraduate half a century ago

British Library Cataloguing-in-Publication Data
A catalogue record for this book is available from the British Library

ISBN 978-0-86140-496-4

Text prepared by Alison Wiblin
Designed by Libanus Press, Marlborough
Printed by Hampton Printing (Bristol) Ltd

CONCERTS AT KING'S 2014–2015

Artistic Director: Stephen Cleobury

The first performance of *Eight Sonnets* by Francis Warner was given
in the hall of King's College, Cambridge, 14 June 2015,
on the occasion of the retirement of the College Chaplain
Richard Lloyd Morgan, and sung by him
with David Goode at the piano.

EIGHT SONNETS

~ 1 ~   *Sometimes a summer's day begins in mist*   13

~ 2 ~   *I did not see the bombs fall on the Thames*   19

~ 3 ~   *Was it mere chance that brought the mating hare*   25

~ 4 ~   *Should we preserve intensity alone*   29

~ 5 ~   *Night wins. The realizing dark*   33

~ 6 ~   *Just now is dawn, and I am out of doors*   37

~ 7 ~   *Twenty-eight fighter bombers overhead*   41

~ 8 ~   *The held cascade of vaulting stone unites*   47

❧ 1 ❧

Sometimes a summer's day begins in mist
And light's expectancy unwraps the trees
Raising the grass to green from amethyst
And whitening soft bird-song melodies.
Heart-lifting certainty the gleam will spread
Irradiates each nerve and every leaf
Across day's blue dominion when the shed
Darkness dissolves and splendour conquers grief.
Opening eyes see all creation waits.
Richness arrives, outlined in early dawn.
Everywhere certainty anticipates
Youth's wild fulfilment as our love is born.

    On comes our day, our lifetime of delight
    Unhurt and marvellous as morning light.

❧ 2 ❧

I did not see the bombs fall on the Thames,
But I did feel next morning's cranes of fire
Each side our boat. My bones seemed to perspire
As buildings yelled skeletal requiems,
Roared, cracked, exploded through the wind's whiplash,
And leaping flames, black smoke, framed Tower Bridge.
My father hoped our Lambeth ferriage
For Temple to St Paul's was not too rash . . .
Day rockets! We turned back. Nazis return
Again each night. Godmother will feed me.
Mother near home with baby on her knee,
Bombed out, is no more safe than us. All burn.

    I slipped. He lifted me. Down my lip curled.
    This surely is the ending of the world.

3

Was it mere chance that brought the mating hare
Almost to touching distance as you stood
Still as a tree beside the sunlit wood
Downwind of him, your beagle nowhere near?
Were the white streaks along his whiskered cheeks
Furrows, too, caused by solitary tears?
Did his loose lope, his absence of all fears
Delight you? All his muddy scattering freaks?
Didn't you feel a happy naturalness
When his doe crossed the harrow to his side?
That all our spring is blest, and has not died –
That deep love triumphs over danger's stress?
  Wasn't this vision in your saddest hours
  An emblem, darling, of what might be ours?

4

Should we preserve intensity alone?
The string vibrating at the 'cello's bridge?
Or stretch to nerve the fingerboard's full range
In orchestrating waste's cacophonics?
Is poignancy of beauty's transience
As time runs over an apple in the stream –
The hesitancy of a summer's dusk
When night-stock stuns with scent – ours to forgo?
Must we desert court-ladies on the grass,
Their sunlit-dappled breasts and lovers' lutes?
The skill of craftsman-wrought, firm, rounded themes;
The guests of Mozart, Purcell, and Watteau?
  Bear with me if I leave such scenes behind:
  The dark offstage preoccupies my mind.

Night wins. The realizing dark
Granites that knife along eternity.
Who sins? What is this idle guilt?
Father forgive, by Thy Gethsemane.
Eat, drink, riot today and forget!
By Thine agony and bloody sweat –
Come, try at the wheel; spin, wager a bet!
Ransom my core from catastrophic debt.
If I must live with this full-earned abyss,
If I must face my moral holocaust,
Father, forgive, though I know what I do,
Forgive my sin against the Holy Ghost.

 The worst is done; the last brutality:
 And mine the sole responsibility.

Just now is dawn, and I am out of doors
Where black-cowled figures glide through flowerless days,
And walk where acorned, herb-filled peace restores
Healing to sadness, green paths through our ways.
Here, as the tiptoed granite mountains rise
Through the September berries, all my heart
And surging thoughts, like sun-gleamed dragonflies,
Bless our touch, half a century apart.
There clangs the bell above the cloistered calm
As startled birds disturb the rosemary
Drifting your nine-years' beauty to my arm,
Leaving your trusting absence close to me.

 Dawn on the leaves turns green to yellow-gold.
 Know that I loved you, when my tale is told.

Twenty-eight fighter bombers overhead
Swooped up our flight path, low, seeking our schools.
Where were the sirens, anti-aircraft tools –
Radar – when we were queuing to be fed?
Minutes south of us, Petworth School last term
Was blasted. Boys and teachers in mass graves
Frost the raw grief. Outside a Junior waves
And is machine-gunned. You, in rubble, squirm
And lose both of your legs. Your playground fills
With sad tarpaulins. Far in the Azores
Your brother Ken's torpedoed. Without oars
They last on their raft two weeks, till thirst kills.
    Quiet, we know – our deaths not far away –
    Love is life's only pulse from dark to day.

The held cascade of vaulting stone unites
Two roses in the Tudor white and red.
See! Every soaring window's highest lights
Demand, undimmed, that no more blood be shed.
The spacious grandeur of this house of God,
Dreamed by a saint, heals internecine blows:
Where seventh Henry's filial steps have trod
Beaufort portcullis joins the Tudor rose.
True, the next Henry set his feet astride
The airy music to enlarge our eyes,
Carved sad initials on his screen, and died,
But we are heirs of all that enterprise;
    Still reconciled by men of lifted view.
    Lord, let not England fall again in two.

The Poet writes

These eight sonnets (strictly formal, though sometimes the rhymes are brought in from the end of lines, usually to the centre) have been selected from a large number written over the years to offer in their new context an outline of the poet's spiritual journey.

SONNET ONE

It opens in peacetime, 1937, with his parents' happiness, and the birth of their newest baby. His father, Hugh, was Vicar of St Andrew's Church, Bishop-thorpe, a small village containing the palace of the Archbishop of York.

Hugh was also Personal Chaplain to William Temple, the Archbishop, a position he was to hold until Temple's death when Archbishop of Canterbury in October 1944. Temple, Godfather to Andrew, the poet's two-year-old elder brother, baptised the new baby from the arms of the Godmother, Temple's own wife Frances.

SONNET TWO

The intensity of the Nazi onslaught on London during the summer and autumn of 1944, with rockets by day and bombers by night, can be glimpsed as experienced by Lambeth Palace in a letter from William Temple, now Archbishop of Canterbury, to the Archbishop of York on 26 July. 'On no night was it possible to look forward to undisturbed rest, and Temple took to sleeping on a sofa in the ground floor passage of the palace . . . He wrote:

> The flying bombs have been falling rather near here lately: there was one at the end of the garden which broke all our windows on that side of the house and some others. . . but last Friday morning there was one just across Lambeth Road . . . which blew in all the windows facing that way as well as a good many others, and shook down several ceilings; it blasted the back door clean off its hinges on to the ground and it jammed the front door and the big gates in

Morton's Tower so they would not open (that is still true of the big gates)...'

F. A. Iremonger, *William Temple*, O.U.P. 1948, p 619.

Hugh, now Vicar of Epsom, took Francis with him to Lambeth, where the Archbishop was ill, to give his mother respite from him after a near-miss had blasted the windows from their home, Epsom Vicarage. Though the two elder brothers had been evacuated, Nancy his mother still had his younger brother, Martin, and baby sister to care for as well as Francis.

In the event of Hugh and Nancy being killed the Temples, who had no children of their own, had agreed, as Godparents, to adopt Andrew and Francis. This visit was therefore an opportunity for Mrs Temple to come to know her Godchild a little better.

On the day this sonnet recalls, the only way messages could reach St Paul's Cathedral from the Archbishop was by the river bus. After what they had been through, Hugh had hoped this boat-trip might have been his son's treat.

SONNET THREE
Adolescence.

SONNET FOUR
Early maturity.

SONNET FIVE
No longer an innocent child victim of war, the mature poet has to confront the evil and moral compromises that come with adult responsibility in himself.

SONNET SIX
Recovery in the Abbaye St Benoît d'En Calcat, the monastery of the silent Benedictine order in Dourgne, southern France, in whose gardens herbs, not flowers, are cultivated. The high standard of the singing of plainchant here (in which he participated) was the reason for his choice of this sanctuary. It is the bell for Laudes, 6.20 a.m. that summons him in line 9.

His mother had just died; and to cheer his austerity his nine-year-old daughter had just sent him a drawing to pin up in his cell.

SONNET SEVEN

The shared return of childhood nightmares in old age. The poet is talking to his friend Mrs Molly Linn, née Kinnuman, who at the age of twelve had lost both her legs in the Sandhurst Road School, Catford, massacre of 1943 by a Nazi plane that two minutes before had flown over the poet's own school seeking children.

SONNET EIGHT

King Henry VI was aged 19 when he laid the first stone of King's College, Cambridge, on Passion Sunday 1441. He returned to lay the foundation stone of his new chapel at the high altar on St James's Day, 25 July 1446. As the building grew during the Wars of the Roses (c.1455–87) it gradually became a symbol of the reconciliation, following the Yorkist defeat, of the warring parties, a reconciliation represented by the Tudor rose, blending the white rose of York with the red rose of Lancaster.

The chapel's magnificent early stained glass completed in 1547 contains many Tudor roses, nearly all of them white surrounded by red, in many of the highest 'lights'.

This sonnet was written during the UK miners' strike of 1984–5.

The Composer writes

After the intense experience of preparing *Blitz Requiem* for performance in September 2013, it seemed a moment to take stock. Accordingly 2014 was deliberately a somewhat fallow year, occupied mainly with typesetting and proof-reading. However, performing *Dichterliebe* during this period, with a group of boys at Eton, had already planted a seed: how pleasurable to feel Schumann's keyboard textures under one's fingers, not to mention hearing the unbridled lyricism of the music as a whole! Might a song-cycle not be fun to write one day, perhaps? So when Francis chose this moment to propose *Eight Sonnets* as a present to Richard Lloyd Morgan, on the occasion of his retirement from King's, the ground was to some extent prepared.

I allowed myself to respond pretty closely to the wide range of moods of the poems. A small linking thread is the 'fanning out' of the vocal line at the beginning of several of the songs. Although much of the tonality is fluid, there is also an underlying key-scheme of interlocking fourths – F sharp, B, A, D (loosely), C minor, F, E flat minor – with the last song breaking the pattern to rise an extra tone to B flat.

Sonnet 1 emerges rhapsodically from the mists of morning; 2 is a nightmarish barcarolle, with two brief trios as family are mentioned. The third begins in recitativo secco, evoking stillness, but warming gradually into lyricism. In Sonnet 4, the structure of an aria enclosed by recitative was suggested by the poem.

Sonnet 5 presents a dialogue: a suggestion of popular genres for the seductive tempter's voice, and solemn declamation for the other (reminiscent of *Gerontius*?). Darkness clears for Sonnet 6, in which modality and a suggestion of plainsong in the melodic lines evoke the tranquillity and austerity of monastic life. Sonnet 7 is a dissonant toccata, becoming elegiac, with a suggestion of hope at the end. From it proceeds the serene hymn of Sonnet 8, complete with gently clanging bells, as the Chapel of King's is held out as an emblem of reconciliation and hope.

❧ SONNET ONE ❧

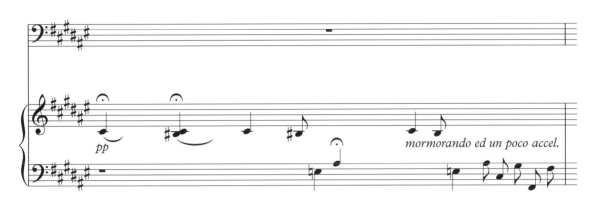

mormorando ed un poco accel.

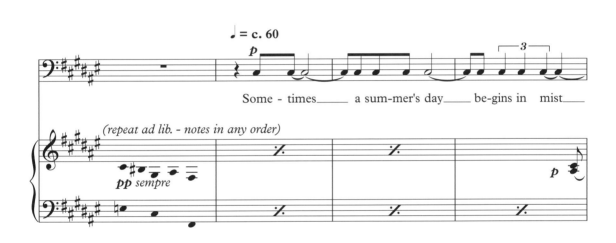

♩ = c. 60

Some - times⸺ a sum-mer's day⸺ be-gins in mist⸺

(repeat ad lib. - notes in any order)

pp sempre

poco cresc.

And light's ex - pect-an - cy⸺ un - wraps the

(becoming gradually measured)

13

trees _____ Rais - ing the grass _____ to green from am - e - thyst And whit - en - ing _____ soft _____ bird-song me-lo - dies. _____ Heart - lift - ing _____

cer-tain-ty the gleam will spread

Ir - rad - i - ates each nerve and ev - ery leaf

A - cross day's blue

do - mi - nion when the shed Dark-ness dis - solves and

15

splen____ dour con-quers grief.   Op - en - ing   eyes____

____ see   all   cre - a - tion   waits.

Rich - ness   ar - rives,_____   out - lined____

____ in   ear - ly   dawn.   Eve - ry - where

cer-tain-ty___ an - ti-ci-pates Youth's___ wild ful - fil - ment___ as our

love is born. On comes our

day, our life - time of de - light_____

Un-hurt and mar - vel-lous as

rit.

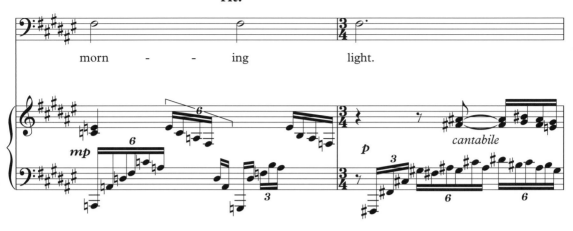

morn – – ing light.

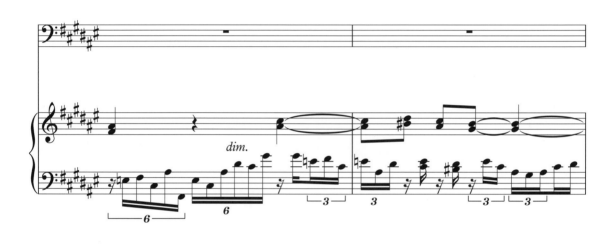

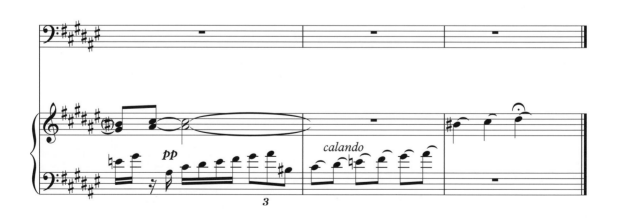

❧ SONNET TWO ❧

With intensity ♩ = 66

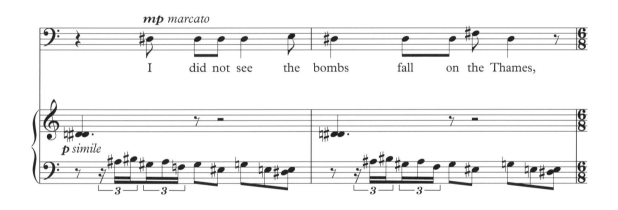

I did not see the bombs fall on the Thames,

But I did feel next mor-ning's cranes_____ of fire

Each side our boat.

My bones   seemed to per-spire   As build- ings yelled   ske - le - tal

re-qui-ems,   Roared,   cracked,

ex-plo- ded____ through the wind's   whip-lash,   And

20

leap - - ing flames,

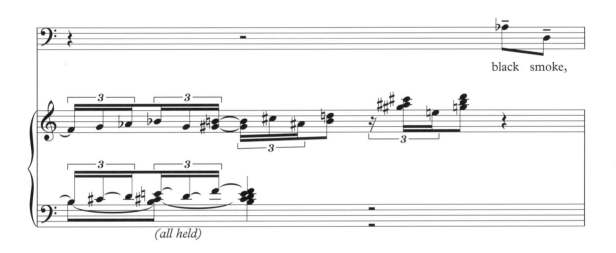

black smoke,

(all held)

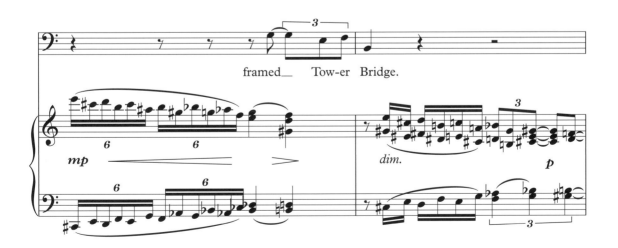

framed__ Tow-er Bridge.

My fa-ther hoped our Lam-beth fer-ri - age___ For Tem-ple to___ St. Paul's was not too rash.... Day rock-ets! We turned back.

I slipped. He lif – ted me. Down my lip curled. This sure-ly is the end - ing of the world.

SONNET THREE

Was it mere chance

that brought the mat-ing hare _ Al - most to touch-ing dis - tance _

_ as you stood Still _ as a tree _ be - side the

sun-lit wood Down-wind of him,__ your beag-le no-where near?

Were__ the white streaks__ a-long his whis-kered cheeks_ Fur-rows,__

__ too,__ caused__ by so-li-ta-ry tears?__ Did his loose lope,__

__ his ab-sence of all fears_ De-light you? All_____ his

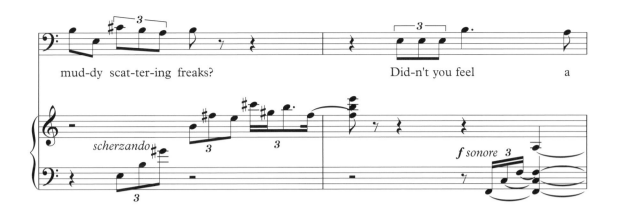

mud-dy scat-ter-ing freaks? Did-n't you feel a

hap-py nat-ural- ness___ When_ his doe crossed the har-row to his side?

That all our spring is blest,___ and has not died — That deep love

tri- umphs___ o - ver dang-er's stress? Was-n't this vi- sion

in___ your sad-dest hours___ An emb - lem, dar -ling,___ of what

might be ours?

SONNET FOUR

Should we pre-serve in-ten-si-ty a-lone? The
string vi-brat-ing at the 'cel-lo's bridge? Or stretch
to nerve the fin-ger board's full range
In orch-es-tra-ting waste's ca-ca-phon-ics?

a tempo

Is poig-nan-cy of beau-ty's tran-si-ence
As time runs ov-er an ap-ple in the stream — The he-si-tan-cy of a
sum-mer's dusk When night-stock stuns with scent — ours to forgo? Must we des-ert court lad-ies on the grass, Their

sun - lit dapp-led breasts and lov - ers' lutes? The skill__ of crafts-man-wrought, firm, round-ed themes; The guests of Moz-art, Pur- cell, and___ Wat- teau? Bear with me if___ I leave such scenes be-hind: The dark off- stage___ pre-oc-cu-pies my mind.

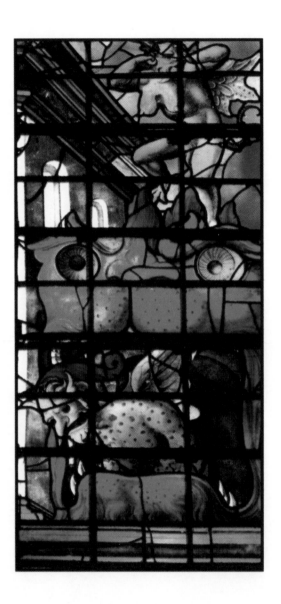

❧ SONNET FIVE ❧

Darkly (♩ = c.70)

Night wins. The re - a - liz-ing dark

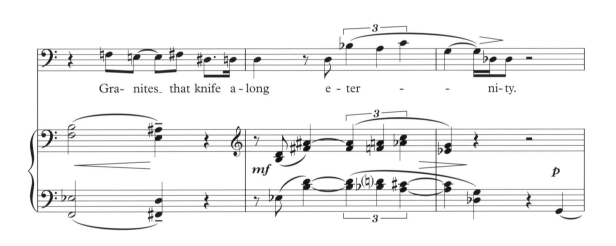

Gra- nites_ that knife a - long e - ter - ni-ty.

Who sins? What is this id - le guilt?_ Fa - ther

for-give,   by Thy Geth - se - ma - ne.

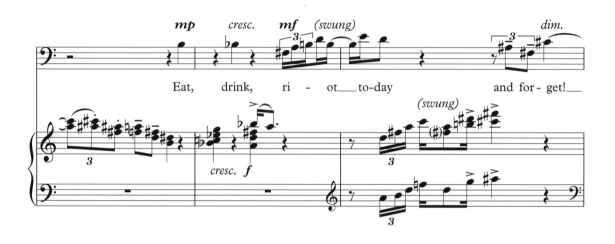

Eat,   drink,   ri - ot___to-day   and for - get!___

___ By Thine a - go - ny   and blood-y sweat__ — Come,   try at the

wheel;   spin,_____   wa-ger a bet!   Ran - som my core

____ from ca - ta - stroph - ic debt.   If____ I must live   with this full-earned a -

byss,   If I must face____ my mo - ral ho - lo-

caust,   Fa - ther, for-give,   though I know what I do.   For-give my

sin a - gainst____ the Ho - ly Ghost.   The worst is

done;   the last___ bru -ta-li-ty: And mine the sole___ res-pon-si-

-bi - li - ty.

❧ SONNET SIX ❧

♩ = 58-60

p sotto voce, sostenuto

Just now is dawn, and

simile

I am out of doors Where black - cowled

fig - ures___ glide___ through flo-wer-less days, And walk___

mp

where a-corned, herb - filled peace re-stores Heal-ing

to sad - ness, green paths through our ways.

Here, as the tip - toed gran-ite mount-ains rise

Through the Sep - tem - ber ber-ries, all my heart

And sur - ging thoughts, like sun - gleamed dra- gon- flies,

Bless__ our touch,_____ half_____ a cen -tu - ry a - part.

There_____ clangs the bell_____ a - bove the clois -tered calm__

___ As star - tled birds dis - turb the rose- ma - ry__ Drift - ing__ your

nine - years' beau-ty__ to my arm, Lea -ving__ your trust-ing abs-ence__ close to

me. Dawn on the leaves_____ turns

green to yel-low gold. Know that I loved you,_ when my

tale is told.

SONNET SEVEN

Twen - ty-eight fight - er bomb - ers

Min-utes south of us, Pet-worth School last term Was blast-ed.

poco meno mosso

Boys and teach-ers in mass graves Frost the raw grief. Out-side a Ju-ni-or waves And is ma-chine-gunned.

You, in rub-ble, squirm_____ And lose both of your legs. Your play-ground fills_____ With sad tar-pau-lins. Far in the A-zores Your bro-ther Ken's _____tor-pe-doed. With-out oars They

last on their raft two weeks, till thirst kills.

Qui-et, we know — our deaths not far a-way — Love is life's on-ly pulse from dark to day.

attacca

❧ SONNET EIGHT ❧

Moderato sostenuto (♩ = 56)

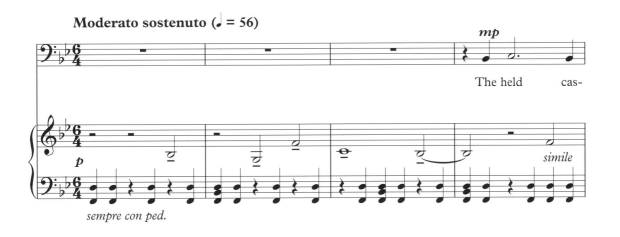

The held cas-

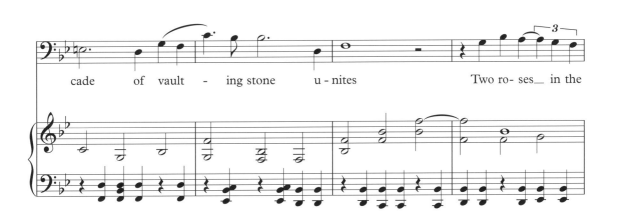

cade of vault - ing stone u - nites   Two ro- ses__ in the

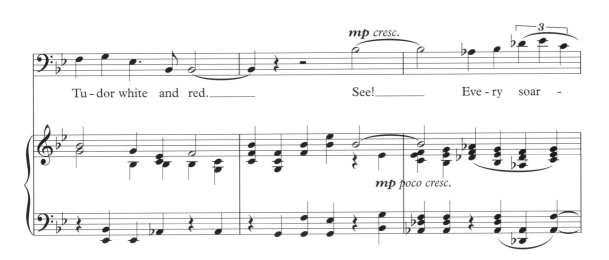

Tu - dor white and red._____   See!_____   Eve - ry soar -

- ing wind-ow's high - est lights   De - mand,   un - dimmed,

that no more blood be shed.   The spa-cious grand- eur_

_   of____ this house of God,____ Dreamed____ by a saint,   heals

in - ter - ne - cine blows: Where____ sev-enth Hen-ry's

fil - ial steps have trod Beau-fort port-cul - lis joins the Tud - or rose.

sostenuto

True, the next Hen - ry___ set his feet a - stride The air -

- - ry mu - sic___ to en-large our eyes,___ Carved sad in -

dim.

it - ials___ on his screen and died, But we are heirs___ of all___

cresc.

49

that en - ter-prise;   Still   re - con - ciled by men   of

lif-ted view.   Lord,   let   not Eng - land fall___

___ a - gain in   two.___

FRANCIS WARNER, M.A., D.Litt., Hon. D.Mus., born 1937, is Emeritus Fellow of St Peter's College, Oxford, and Residential Honorary Fellow of St Catharine's College, Cambridge, where in the 1950s he was a Choral Exhibitioner. Educated at Christ's Hospital and the London College of Music, at Cambridge he conducted his own re-scoring of Honegger's *King David* in King's College Chapel for two performances in 1958. In 2003 the recording of this concert was issued as a Landmark Recording CD by OxRecs Digital (OXCD–94).

Sixteen of his plays, his *Collected Poems 1960–1984*, *Nightingales: Poems 1985–1996*, and *By the Cam and the Isis 1954–2000* (two long poems) are published by Colin Smythe Ltd, who also publishes *Six Anthems* by David Goode and Francis Warner (with accompanying CD of King's College Choir under Stephen Cleobury singing all six anthems in their liturgical context), and also their *Blitz Requiem* performed by the Bach Choir with the Royal Philharmonic Orchestra in St Paul's Cathedral, London, September 2013 commemorating the 70th anniversary of the Blitz and subsequent five years aerial bombardment of the British Isles.

David Goode

DAVID GOODE was born in 1971 and was educated as a music scholar at Eton College and as organ scholar at King's College, Cambridge, where he took a double First in Music and subsequently the MPhil. in Musicology. He was Sub-Organist at Christ Church, Oxford, where he also tutored; while there he wrote his first piece, *Like as the Hart*, for the cathedral choir. Having won several prizes at the 1997 St Alban's and 1998 Calgary Organ Competitions, he was a freelance performer and teacher between 2001 and 2003, touring internationally and appearing at UK festivals such as the BBC Proms and the Aldeburgh Festival.

Between 2003 and 2005 he was Organist in Residence at First Congregational Church in Los Angeles, with performances of his works including those by the brass of the LA Philharmonic. His *Concert Fantasy on themes by Gershwin*, written for the new organ of Symphony Hall, Birmingham in 2002, has achieved some popularity. Since 2005 he has been Organist (and until recently Head of Keyboard) at Eton College, combining this full-time position with a continuing concert and recording career.

His collaboration with Francis Warner began in 2003 when the Choir of King's College performed *Anthem for St Cecilia's Day*; that partnership now numbers 6 anthems, a carol and a set of organ variations, all variously performed in Oxford, Cambridge and Eton, and recorded by King's with OxRecs Digital. *Blitz Requiem* was performed by the Bach Choir and RPO under David Hill at St Paul's Cathedral in 2013, and broadcast on Classic FM.

Richard Lloyd Morgan

RICHARD LLOYD MORGAN had a career of over 25 years as a concert and opera singer before taking up a vocation to the priesthood. He made his major European debut in Berlin in 1987 as Nick Shadow in *The Rake's Progress*, and returned to sing several roles, most notably Mittenhofer in Henze's *Elegy For Young Lovers* and William in Philip Glass's *The Fall of the House of Usher*.

In 1989 he sang the title role in *Nabucco* for the Chelsea Opera Group, and was then invited to sing for several major European houses, including Glyndebourne, Opera North, Scottish Opera and Covent Garden, for whom he made his debut as Yamadori in *Madame Butterfly* in 1992.

He has also performed at festivals world-wide, including Hong Kong, Athens and the Maggio Musicale in Florence. He has sung in Japan with the Tokyo Philharmonic and performed recitals of *Die schöne Müllerin* in the Gulf States, Nairobi and Cape Town. In 1995 he visited Argentina, Spain and Finland with Trevor Pinnock, singing in a production of *King Arthur*, and in 2000 he toured Borneo with recitals of English and American songs. At La Monnaie in Brussels he sang a Flemish Deputy in *Don Carlos* with Pappano, and Ceprano in *Rigoletto* under Jurovski. At the ROH he sang Ping in its production of *Turandot* and Konrad Nachtigall in *Die Meistersinger* under Bernard Haitink.

For Scottish Opera he has sung the roles of Abimelech in *Samson and Delilah* and Baron Douphol in *La Traviata*. For Scottish Opera Go Round, he sang the title role in *Don Pasquale* and the Father in *Hansel and Gretel*. His Amsterdam debut was with the Nederlandse Opera in Vivier's *Kopernikus*, a work that breaks many operatic moulds.

In 2002 he sang the title role in Maxwell Davies's *Mr Emmet Takes a Walk* and in the same year sang Père Germont in *La Traviata* for Holland Park Opera, returning in 2003 as Le Bailli in *Werther*.

Richard was Chaplain of King's College, Cambridge, from 2003 to 2015. At King's he took part in many concerts, including recitals of *Winterreise* and *Die schöne Müllerin*, and in May also gave a farewell cabaret concert in this year's *Concerts at King's* series.